Encyclopedia of Plants, Fungi, and Lichens

for Young Readers

Albatros

CONTENTS

FLOWERING PLANTS

We're a varied group.

We're big and small.

We grow attractive flowers.

Our stems are woody and juicy.

This is a highly varied group of plants. Surprisingly, we find in it a tiny flowering plant called the wolffia, as well as giant trees. Woody plants, which are comprised of trees and shrubs, have a wooden stem. Herbs are plants with a pulpy (soft) stem. Plants produce flowers to ensure their survival. Colorful, fragrant flowers in particular attract insects, which pollinate them, thereby allowing them to produce seeds. And it is mostly seeds—of all shapes, colors, and sizes—that serve to reproduce.

✳ Black bamboo

A remarkable grass, bamboo makes up much of a giant panda's diet. Some of its canes grow very quickly from the start. Meanwhile, we hear the bursting of germinating shoots. Yes, we really can hear grass grow!

✳ Roselle

This plant grows in tropical regions all over the world. Its Latin name, *hibiscus*, refers to the ibis, a sacred bird of the Ancient Egyptians. Its flowers and its red, pulpy calyxes are used to make teas, syrups, jellies, and jams.

✳ Sensitive plant

When touched, this sensitive plant folds in its leaflets until the whole leaf is hidden. When the touch is severe—in heavy rain or high winds, for instance—the whole plant withdraws and takes on a dried-up appearance.

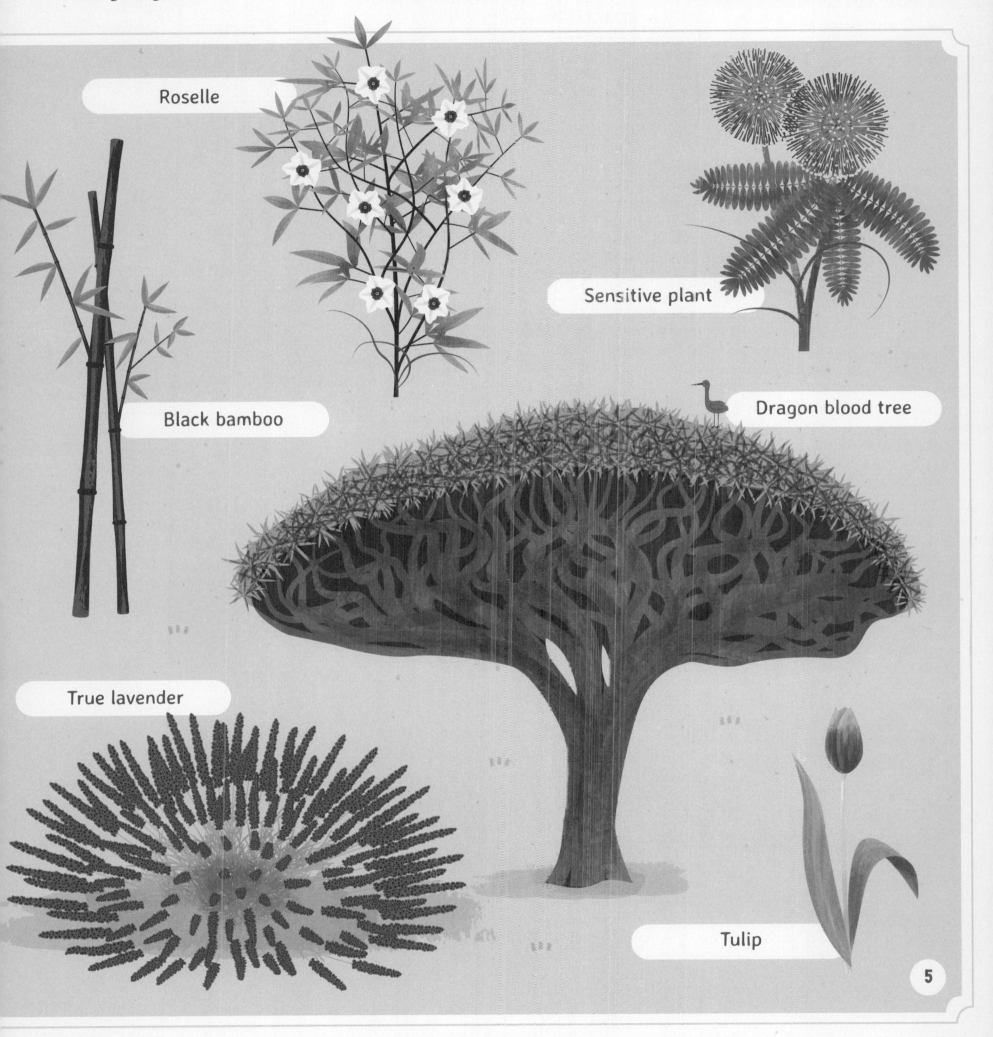

Roselle

Sensitive plant

Black bamboo

Dragon blood tree

True lavender

Tulip

✳ True lavender

Because of its fragrance and soothing qualities, lavender has been added to baths since ancient times. It is included in cosmetic products. And as it repels insects, people sometimes put it in their wardrobes to repel clothes moths.

✳ Dragon blood tree

When injured, the trunk or a branch of this tree releases a reddish-brown resin known as dragon blood. In the past, it was much used in folk medicine, as a dye or in the production of varnish.

✳ Tulip

Tulips are the world's most famous bulbous plants. More than anywhere else, they are grown in the Netherlands. Tulips come in a huge range of colors—perhaps only blue and black are not represented.

5

Conifers

Coniferous trees are very old plants. Their acerose (needle-shaped) leaves are covered with a hard, thick skin that prevents the excessive evaporation of water. With a few exceptions, conifers are evergreen, meaning that the tree keeps its leaves (needles) all year round. In most cases, the fruit is a cone, although some conifers instead have colored berries.

Silver fir

Scots pine

Monkey puzzle tree

Mediterranean cypress

✴ Monkey puzzle tree

This tree is one of the oldest woody plants on the planet. Its prickly, scale-like, dark-green leaves are arranged around the branches in spirals, and the trunk is dotted with them too.

✴ Silver fir

This conifer is sensitive to air pollution. The cones on its branches grow upward. After ripening, they decompose on the tree. Resistant to water, the wood of the fir tree is often used in hydraulic engineering.

✴ Mediterranean cypress

As the cypress can retain a lot of water, it has excellent fire-resistant properties. Cypress wood is hard and durable. In Ancient Egypt, it was used for the sarcophagi of Pharaohs.

Scots pine

Pine trees need lots of light. One of the uses of their resin is in the production of rosin, which is applied to the bridges of musical instruments, so that they hold closer to the strings during playing.

European larch

Thinner branches hang from the powerful main branches of the European larch, with needles arranged in bunches growing on them. The cones stay on the tree for several years.

Norway spruce

The Norway spruce has short, prickly needles. Unlike fir cones, spruce cones hang from the branch. Spruce is used to produce furniture, musical instruments, and paper.

European larch

Norway spruce

California redwood

Common yew

Japanese umbrella pine

California redwood

The redwood is a giant of the plant kingdom. In fact, it is the world's tallest tree! It can grow to be up to 380 feet tall and live to a great age. Standing next to a redwood, you will feel like an ant.

Japanese umbrella pine

The umbrella pine grows in mountainous regions of Japan. Its long needles grow at the end of shoots and are arranged in an umbrella shape.

Common yew

With the exception of the fleshy red arils, out of which the seed peeks, the entire plant is extremely poisonous. In the past, crossbows and longbows were made from the wood of the yew.

Deciduous trees

Deciduous trees have many different kinds of broad, flat leaves. In tropical, subtropical, and dry regions, they lose their leaves in the dry season. In temperate climates, deciduous trees lose their leaves in autumn. In the process, the color of their leaves often changes from green to yellow, orange, brown, or red.

Grandidier's baobab

Rainbow eucalyptus

Silver birch

Cacao tree

Java cotton

✻ Rainbow eucalyptus

The colorful trunk of the rainbow eucalyptus is painted by nature, not humans. Peeling strips of bark from the tree reveals phloem—which are like its veins and arteries—of various colors.

✻ Silver birch

The trunk of the young silver birch is covered with white bark, which peels off in thin layers. There are black marks on the trunk of an old tree. Holes are drilled into the trunk to collect birch water, which is used in cosmetics.

✻ Cacao tree

First the flowers then the fruit of this small tree grow directly on its trunk. The fruit contain seeds—cocoa beans, which are used to make cocoa powder and chocolate.

✳ Grandidier's baobab

The baobab is the greatest beast of the tree world. This is because its trunk can hold a great deal of water. In the dry season, having shed its leaves, it looks as though it is standing on its head, with its roots in the air.

✳ Banyan fig

This tree has a strange way of growing. It forms aerial roots, which grow downward from its branches. Over time they come to look like secondary trunks supporting the ever-growing crown.

✳ Small-leaved lime

The wood of the lime is often used by woodcarvers and sculptors. A lime tree that is in flower is a pasture for bees, which, back in their hives, turn the nectar they gather into linden honey. Linden flower tea is good for coughs and colds.

Small-leaved lime

Banyan fig

Horse chestnut

Cork oak

9

✳ Java cotton

Its strong, tubular roots grow from the trunk in ripples. Fiber taken from its ripe seed pods, known as kapok, is used as stuffing for mattresses and pillows, as a filling for life jackets, and as an insulating material.

✳ Cork oak

The thick bark of the cork oak protects it from water loss and overheating. It is a source of natural cork. Stripped of bark, the tree does not die. Indeed, over time the layer of cork will grow back.

✳ Horse chestnut

Inside the prickly green fruit of the horse chestnut tree is a brown seed, known as a conker. In the past, conkers were grated and used instead of soap.

Shrubs

Like trees, shrubs (bushes) are woody plants. Unlike trees, however, they don't have a central trunk. They branch out at ground level or just above. Most shrubs are shorter than trees but taller than grasses and herbs.

Black elder

Tea plant

Sea buckthorn

Upland cotton

Summer lilac

❋ Tea plant

The top leaves of the tea plant are used to make tea, a drink well known all over the world. The type of tea (most notably black, green, and white tea) depends on the way the leaves are processed after harvesting.

❋ Summer lilac

This plant comes from China. The sweet, heady smell of its purple blooms attracts bumblebees and a great many butterflies.

❋ Sea buckthorn

In autumn, this spiny shrub is laden with orange berries. Filled with vitamins, these berries are used—in compotes, jams, syrups, and many other delicious things—to help the human body resist disease.

✳ Black elder

The elder has many different uses. As a medicinal plant, its dried leaves are used to make tea. Its berries are used to make syrup rich in vitamin C and wine, while its wood is used to produce musical pipes, whistles, and fujaras.

✳ Dog rose

The stems of the dog rose have small hooked prickles, which serve as protection against herbivores. Its pink or white flowers have a pleasant scent. The hip, its fruit, contains vitamins and is used to make tea.

✳ Common snowberry

In autumn, the common snowberry is laden with white berries. If you drop these berries on the ground and stamp on them, they make a popping sound. In winter, the berries are a delicacy sought after by birds.

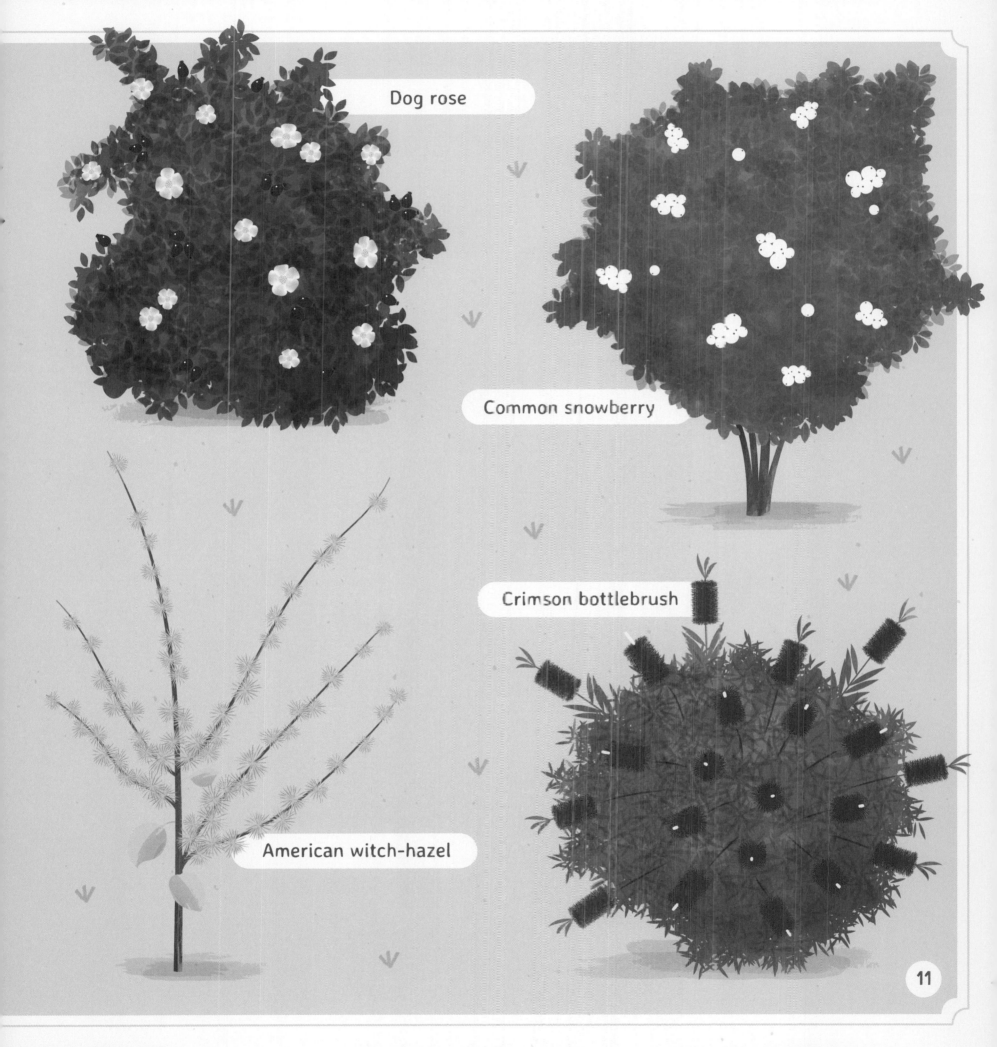

Dog rose

Common snowberry

Crimson bottlebrush

American witch-hazel

11

✳ Upland cotton

After it flowers, the upland cotton produces a fruit that contains a seed covered in fuzz. On ripening, the fruit bursts, revealing a tuft of cotton inside. These tufts are gathered and processed into cotton fiber for textiles.

✳ American witch-hazel

Witch-hazel produces flowers in autumn and winter. When ripe, its fruit shoots its seeds over distances of up to 30 feet. In the past, dowsers used sprigs of witch-hazel in their search for groundwater and mineral riches.

✳ Crimson bottlebrush

The striking red flowers do look like brushes for cleaning bottles. When rubbed, young leaves smell lemony. The fruit of the crimson bottlebrush is a capsule that remains closed until the plant dies or there is a fire.

Palms

Palms, too, are woody plants. They are widespread in tropical and subtropical regions all over the world. Most palms have a simple slender trunk without branches, topped with a tuft of leaves. The trunk bears scars where leaves have fallen. Many palms have important uses—not only are they a source of food, but they also serve as building materials, and they are highly decorative too.

Oil palm

Common rattan

Sea coconut

Doum palm

Ruffled fan palm

12

✳ Common rattan

The rattan has the longest known stem of all plants. This palm and several similar species are used to produce rattan furniture. Most rattan palms are climbing plants with a prickly stem.

✳ Doum palm

The doum palm is found throughout Africa. Unlike most other palms, its trunk branches dichotomously—meaning it divides into two parts. Its fruit has been discovered in the tombs of Egyptian Pharaohs.

✳ Sea coconut

This palm has the largest seed in the plant kingdom, weighing over 40 pounds! Unlike the coconut, it does not float, which explains why the species has never spread beyond its original home, the Seychelles Islands.

✳ Oil palm

The fruit of the oil palm is a rich source of vegetable oil. But the felling of primeval forests to make way for the plantations on which it is grown has a negative effect on the local environment.

✳ Wax palm

The world's tallest palm grows mainly in the misty mountain forests of Colombia. Its strikingly slender trunk has distinctive leaf scars around it and is covered in a layer of wax.

✳ European fan palm

This fan palm is the only indigenous palm species in Europe. In most cases, it forms several stems, giving it a shrub-like character. Its leaves produce a fiber that is used to make mats, sacks, and baskets.

Wax palm

Coconut tree

European fan palm

Date palm

13

✳ Ruffled fan palm

The fan palm boasts beautiful fronds. Growing up to ten feet tall, it occurs naturally in the undergrowth of rainforests, in places where the temperature and humidity are high all year round.

✳ Coconut tree

In shops, we find only the seed of the coconut, stripped of the fibrous pericarp that allows it to float on water. Thanks to this ability, it has traveled great distances, taking root on different islands and continents.

✳ Date palm

This palm is often found in oases. The date, its fruit is more than just popular: it is a staple food in North Africa and the Middle East. Dates are eaten dried as well as fresh. Palm cabbage is prepared from the palm's young leaves.

Succulents & cacti

Their bodies (stem and leaves) can hold large amounts of water—meaning that they can survive long periods of drought. Cacti are among the best-known succulents. They come from the continents of North and South America, although we find them elsewhere too. Most cacti have spines, not leaves.

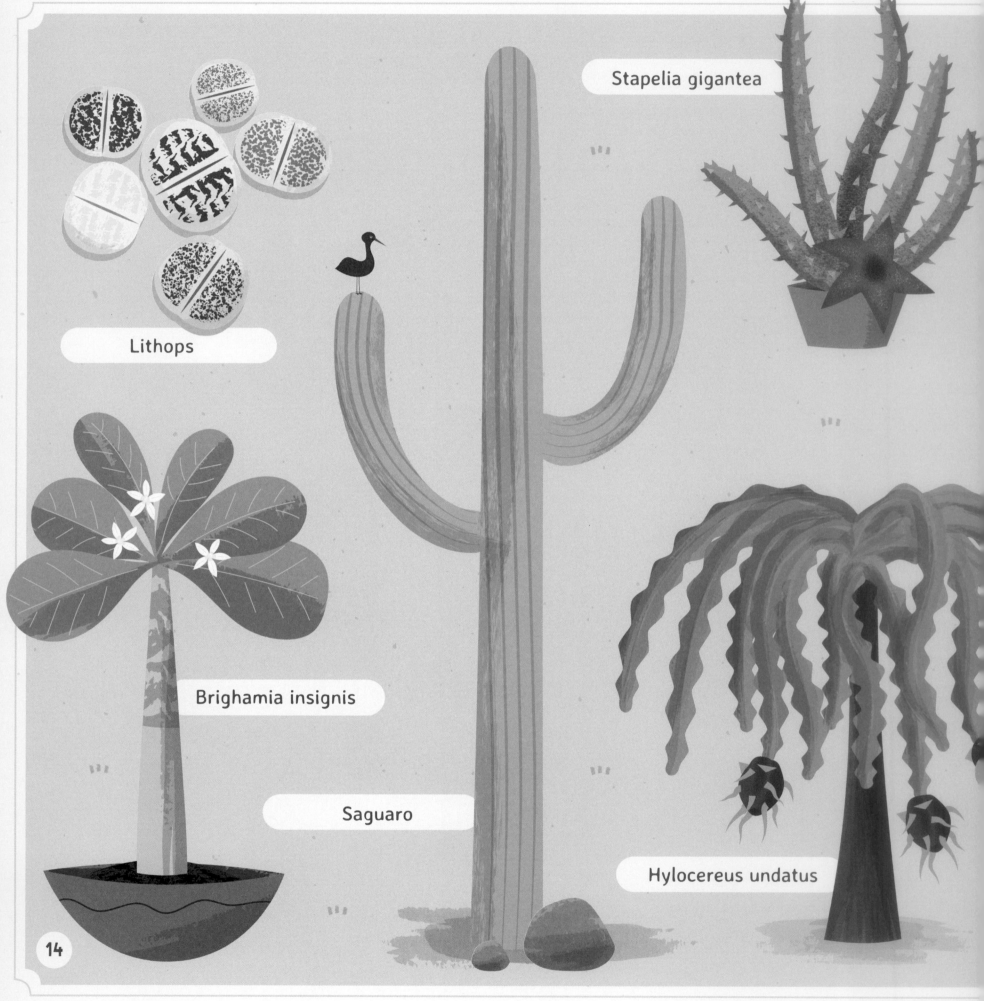

Lithops

Stapelia gigantea

Brighamia insignis

Saguaro

Hylocereus undatus

❋ Lithops

Also known as living stones, lithops take on the shape and color of the real stones around them, so that you can hardly tell them apart. Their small, fleshy bodies are divided in the middle by a narrow opening.

❋ Brighamia insignis

This plant originated on the islands of Hawaii. In all likelihood, it is now extinct in the wild. The species is kept alive, though, in botanical gardens.

❋ Saguaro

The largest species of cactus, the saguaro, can grow to be 50 feet tall! What's more, it can live for 250 years. Some birds peck hollows in the saguaro to nest in it.

✱ Stapelia gigantea

The flower of the stapelia stinks like rotten meat, thereby attracting flies, its main pollinators. A fly often lays its eggs in the middle of the flower, in the mistaken belief that in this place the larvae will find food aplenty.

✱ Aloe vera

Aloe grows in rosettes of fleshy, spike-toothed leaves. Its tubular flowers are mostly pollinated by birds feeding on its nectar. It is used as a medicinal plant.

✱ Agave americana

Its gray-blue leaves can be six feet long. It blooms just once, dying after flowering. The stalk bearing its yellow flowers may grow to be 25 feet tall.

Aloe vera

Agave americana

Cephalocereus senilis

Prickly pear

15

✱ Hylocereus undatus

Its large aromatic flowers bloom for one night only. Following pollination, the red fruit that emerges resembles a lizard or a dragon. This explains why the edible fruit (called pitahaya) is also known as dragon fruit.

✱ Cephalocereus senilis

This tall, slim cactus is at home in Mexico. It is covered with thick white hair, giving it a shaggy appearance and protecting it from the sun's rays.

✱ Prickly pear

This cactus's many flat, prickly surfaces inspire caution, but it has an edible fruit. Cochineal insects feed on the prickly pear by sucking juice from it, thereby turning it red.

Parasitic & carnivorous plants

Commonly, carnivorous plants grow in soil that is low in nutrients. As they often lack nitrogen, they supplement their diet with meat, especially insects, which they hunt. Parasitic plants, on the other hand, are dependent on other plants, which give them the substances they need to develop and grow.

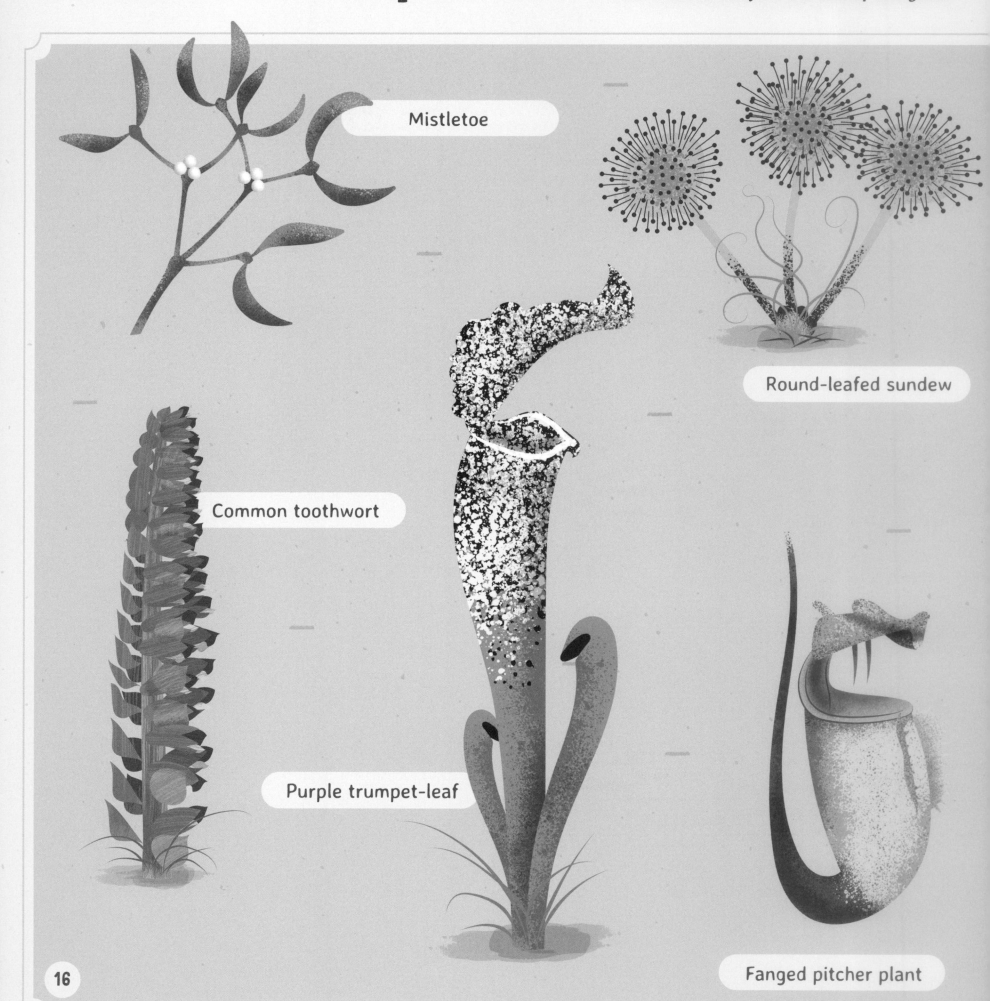

Mistletoe

Round-leafed sundew

Common toothwort

Purple trumpet-leaf

Fanged pitcher plant

❋ Mistletoe

Mistletoe grows on coniferous and deciduous trees. It roots itself in tree bark in order to draw out the water and substances it needs.

❋ Common toothwort

This parasitic plant lives mainly on the roots of deciduous trees. Its pink or pinkish-purple leaves cover the entire stem, from its top to the ground, and even below the ground.

❋ Purple trumpet-leaf

Like the pitcher plant, the trumpet-leaf catches its prey in its pitcher. The traps of some species are up to three feet high. In summer, they are often filled to the brim with insects.

✸ Round-leafed sundew

The leaves of the sundew are covered with small hair-like stalks. The ends of the stalks secrete a sticky slime, which shines in the light like dewdrops. Insects that attach themselves have no chance of escape.

✸ Knapweed broomrape

The thick stem of this pinkish-red and yellow plant ends in a dense bunch of flowers. It is a parasite that lives on chicory roots.

✸ Corpse lily

The corpse lily has the largest flower on Earth. It has a very unpleasant odor and grows in the tropical rainforests of Southeast Asia, where it is parasitic and lives on lianas.

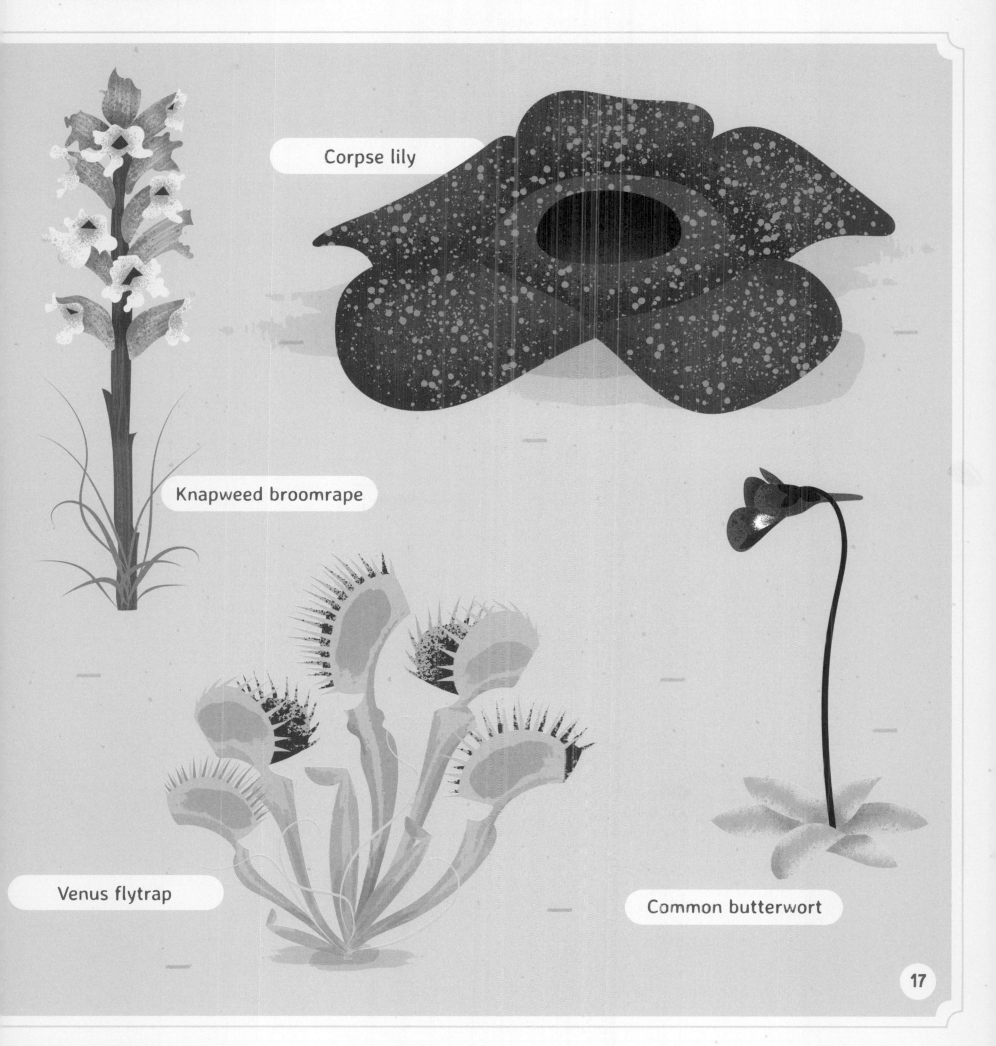

Corpse lily

Knapweed broomrape

Venus flytrap

Common butterwort

17

✸ Fanged pitcher plant

Pitcher plants have liquid traps at the ends of their leaves that look like pitchers. Along their edges is secreted a sweet nectar that attracts insects to their slippery walls. Having slipped down the wall, the prey is drowned.

✸ Venus flytrap

The leaves of the flytrap have a special trapping structure. When, for instance, a fly lands on a leaf, this leaf snaps shut; the pointed protrusions on the leaf's edge prevent the prey from escaping.

✸ Common butterwort

The leaves of the butterwort are covered with a slimy, sticky substance that sparkles in the light, thereby attracting insects. Once the insect is stuck to a leaf, the plant feeds on it by slowly breaking it down.

Creeping plants

They make their way upward by different techniques. Some have outgrowths in the form of roots and suckers, which can attach themselves to tree bark or the wall of a house. Others form bines, which wrap themselves around a support of some kind. Still others twist like snakes, winding themselves around their supports from all sides.

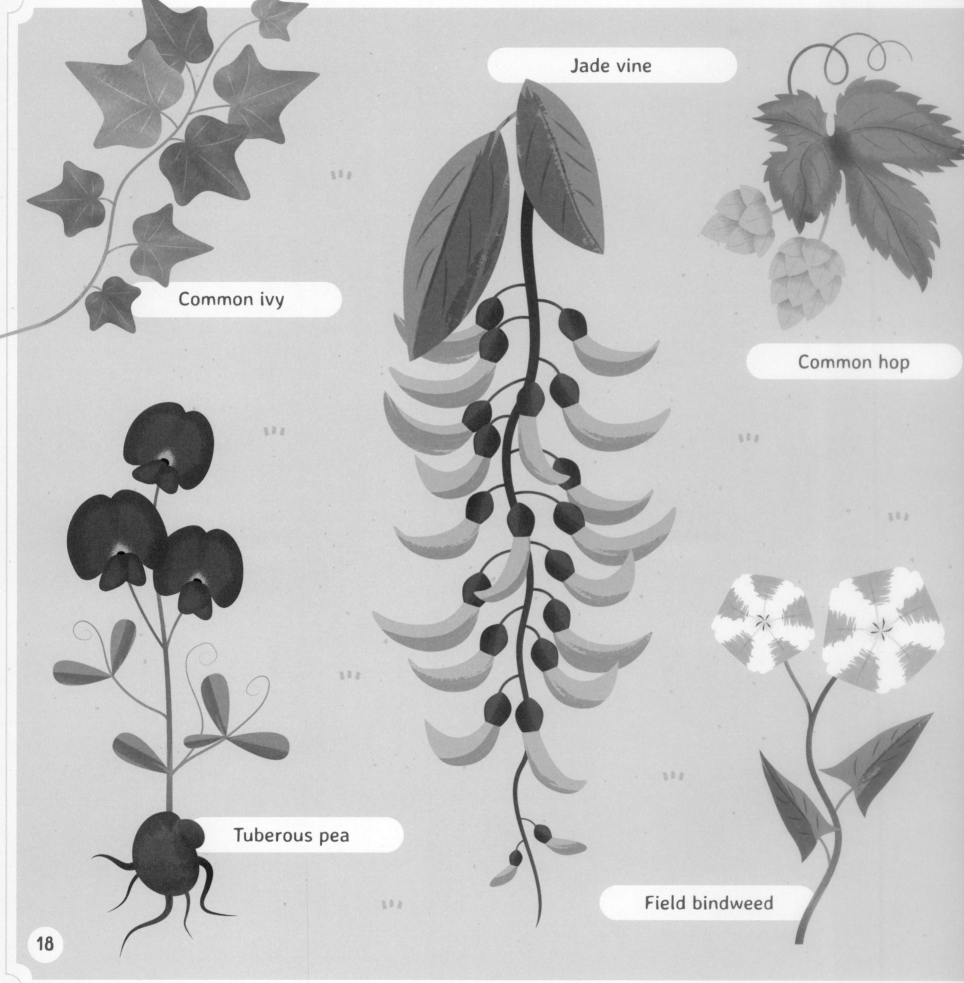

Common ivy

Jade vine

Common hop

Tuberous pea

Field bindweed

18

❋ Common ivy

Ivy is an evergreen plant that can live for several hundred years. It creeps along the ground and climbs up trees or house walls, dressing them in a smart coat.

❋ Tuberous pea

The tuberous pea either just lies around or climbs toward the sun, using other plants for support. Its root tubers may be eaten raw or cooked and have a nutty flavor.

❋ Jade vine

This plant grows in the rainforests of the Philippines. It is unusual in the plant world in that it blooms in huge hanging compound flowers, which are turquoise in color. In the wild, it is pollinated by bats.

✿ Common hop

The hardy rhizome of the common hop is covered in downward-facing hairs that help the plant to climb. An important component in the making of beer, hop cones have a special smell and taste.

✿ Magnolia vine

The magnolia vine, which has striking red berries, comes from Asia. Because of its unmistakable piquancy, in China the magnolia vine is called the plant of five tastes (sour, bitter, sweet, salty, and spicy).

✿ Woodbine

The bines of the woodbine operate as suckers. On contact, they release a glue-like substance that enables the plant to move, even along a very smooth surface. In autumn, its leaves turn red.

Woodbine

Magnolia vine

Giant pelican flower

Passion fruit

19

✿ Field bindweed

Bindweed twists its stems around everything within reach. A weed, it is the torment of every gardener, as it is very difficult to get rid of.

✿ Passion fruit

The passion fruit originated in the tropics and subtropics of the continent of South America. It uses its long, spiral-shaped tendrils to attach itself to trees and other supports. Its fruit (the maracuya) is edible.

✿ Giant pelican flower

The giant pelican flower is at home in South America. The flowers of this liana resemble a piece of raw meat. Their putrid smell attracts insects, which pollinate the plant.

Aquatic & marsh plants

To survive, they need to grow in or near water. Most aquatic plants are rooted firmly in the bed of a body of water, with their leaves and flowers on the surface. But floating plants have all their parts, including the roots, on the surface, while other plants are entirely submerged in water. In places of high humidity, marsh plants can live out of water too.

Water caltrop

Common water hyacinth

Common eelgrass

Indian lotus

❋ Water caltrop

The leaves of the water caltrop remain small until the germinating plant reaches the surface. Then the leaves fall, replaced by larger ones arranged on the water in a rosette shape. Its fruit is an edible horned nut.

❋ Common water hyacinth

Although the purplish flower of the water hyacinth is beautiful, the plant itself causes many problems. It reproduces very quickly to form a dense cover over calm water, causing complications for shipping, for instance.

❋ Common eelgrass

A type of so-called seagrass, this marine flowering plant is forever underwater. These grasses form great underwater meadows for turtles and other creatures to graze on.

❋ Victoria amazonica

As the world's largest water lily, whose huge leaves could hold a baby, it flowers at night for a short time only. On the first evening, its flowers are white. The next evening, the flowers are pink—for the first and last time!

❋ Yellow water lily

Although its thick rhizome wallows in the mud, its large leaves and little yellow flowers float atop the water.

❋ Marsh calla

It grows in woodland pools, muddy, shallow waters, and marshes. Its interesting white flowers give way to bright red berries.

Victoria amazonica

Yellow water lily

Marsh calla

Broadleaf cattail

Lesser duckweed

❋ Indian lotus

Seated on long stems, its flowers stick out of the water. Its leaves are coated in wax, so that rain falls from them very quickly, washing away all dirt.

❋ Lesser duckweed

This floating plant, which looks like little green flakes, grows abundantly in ponds. It spreads to form a green carpet over water.

❋ Broadleaf cattail

This perennial herbaceous plant often grows on the banks of ponds, marshes, and other bodies of water. Its brown inflorescence is reminiscent of a cigar.

Meadow plants

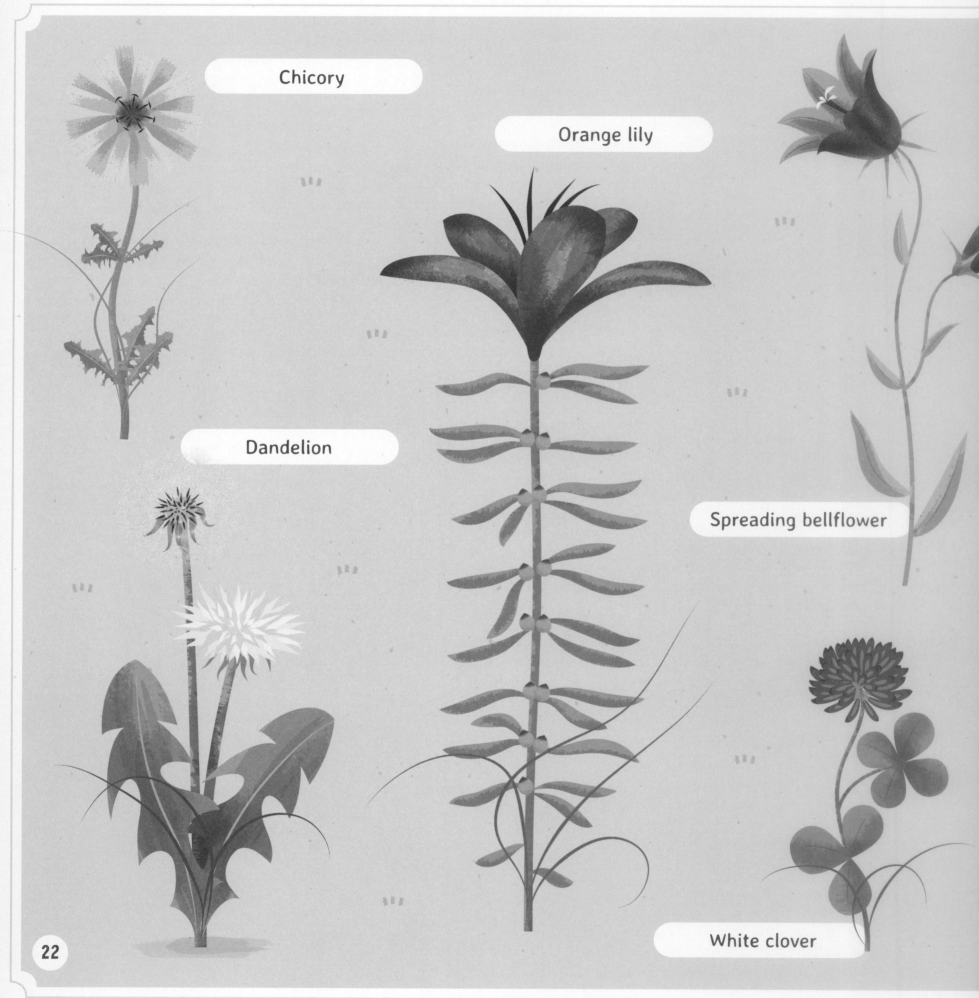

Chicory

Orange lily

Dandelion

Spreading bellflower

White clover

22

✳ Chicory

Chicory was once highly prized for its positive effects on human health. Its roasted root is used as a coffee substitute—and as it contains no caffeine, it is suitable for children too.

✳ Dandelion

When torn, the dandelion oozes a white juice that tastes unpleasantly bitter. After it flowers, white heads of seed-bearing fluff appear. A tiny puff of breath will carry the dandelion a little further on its way.

✳ Orange lily

The orange lily rarely produces seeds. To reproduce, it relies on secondary bulbs near the petals on its stem. Having reached the ground, the small, round bulbs will grow into new plants.

✽ Spreading bellflower

If you decided to track down all of the bellflowers, you would count over 300 species. In most cases, the flower is blue with a purplish hue.

✽ Yarrow

Among other things, the yarrow helps heal wounds and stop bleeding. According to legend, the Greek hero Achilles used it during the Trojan War. It also provides yellow, orange, and brown pigment for the dyeing of wool.

✽ Corn poppy

After ripening, poppy seeds burst through openings in the poppy head at the top of the plant. These seeds do not escape all at once; they do so gradually, as the poppy sways in the wind.

Corn poppy

Yarrow

Elder-flowered orchid

Oxeye daisy

23

✽ White clover

Clover is a food in common use for farm animals. It is characterized by its ball-shaped flowers and three leaflets. If you look hard and are lucky, you might find a rare four-leaf clover.

✽ Oxeye daisy

Grazing cows don't bother much with daisies, eating them only when there is nothing better around. Horses and sheep don't mind them, though. And goats? They actively seek them out.

✽ Elder-flowered orchid

Just as humans have hair of different colors, the flowers of the elderflowered orchid vary in color too. They can be yellow or purple. Both varieties are found in the same habitat. The yellow one, though, is more common.

Poisonous plants

Poisonous plants are widespread—there are surely many of them near where you live. The poisons they contain are various. These plants may be beautiful or unremarkable, and often they look perfectly innocent—but some can be harmful to your health or even deadly. Even so, certain poisonous plants are used both in folk healing and in modern medicine.

Herb-paris

Autumn crocus

Henbane

Lily of the valley

Rosary pea

✱ Henbane

The shaggy henbane has an unpleasant smell. It grows in scrubland and fields and on the roadside. A single plant produces over 8,000 seeds.

✱ Rosary pea

The seeds of the rosary pea are often used as beads to make jewelry and rosaries. Beneath their hard skin, however, these seeds are poisonous. The rest of the plant is harmless.

✱ Lily of the valley

Not only is the plant itself poisonous, but so is water from the vase in which one has been kept. It produces red berries.

✴ Herb-paris

The berries of the herb-paris look like lovely big bilberries. But animals stay away from this plant because of its unpleasant taste and odor.

✴ Garden monkshood

Usually, it grows in mountainous regions, most commonly near a stream. As garden monkshood is easy to find, it became a favorite with poisoners. In the past, it was used, for example, in poisoned arrows.

✴ Deadly nightshade

This whole plant is poisonous. Its bell-shaped flowers produce beautiful, shiny black berries. The poison of the deadly nightshade can be transferred to humans, who consume the flesh or milk of animals that have grazed on it.

Garden monkshood

Deadly nightshade

Hemlock

Castor oil plant

✴ Autumn crocus

The autumn crocus produces flowers in autumn, when it has no leaves. During wintertime, it withdraws into the ground, growing leaves only in the spring.

✴ Castor oil plant

The castor oil plant contains ricin, one of the most toxic of plant poisons. Most ricin is contained in the leaves. As the plant ripens, its fruit bursts and seeds pop out.

✴ Hemlock

This relative of the carrot is extremely toxic. It contains a poison that causes suffocation. In Ancient Greece, a hemlock decoction was used as a means of execution.

Medicinal plants

Medicinal plants are the most important source of natural remedies. Used since time immemorial by folk healers, today they are used by modern medicine too. They contain substances that are good for our health; some of them even have the power to heal. They are used to make teas, syrups, ointments, compresses, and many other useful things.

Chamomile

Maral root

Denseflower mullein

Peppermint

Common soapwort

26

✱ Denseflower mullein

The flower of the denseflower mullein is used to treat coughs. It is also used in the dyeing (yellow, orange, or brown) of fabrics and wool.

✱ Chamomile

Chamomile has a long history as a medicinal herb, and it remains one of the most popular. Its range of uses is so broad that there is practically no area in which chamomile cannot be of some help to us.

✱ Common soapwort

This plant is used medicinally to treat respiratory and skin diseases. Its root contains substances that foam in water, like soap—which explains why it was once used for washing and doing laundry.

✻ Maral root

Maral root comes from southern Siberia, where deer dig up its roots with their hooves before eating them with relish. They are good for the deer's health and help them survive the cruel Siberian winter.

✻ Common sage

Sage leaves contain the most active substances in sunny, dry weather, just before they flower. Uses of these strongly aromatic leaves—fresh and dried—include seasoning for food.

✻ St John's wort

This plant has calming properties. There are black, dye-containing glands on the jagged edges of its yellow flowers. When you rub these in your fingers, they turn your skin red.

St John's wort

Common sage

Purple coneflower

Ginseng

✻ Peppermint

For ages, peppermint has been cultivated for its healing properties—vestiges of peppermint have been found in Ancient Egyptian tombs. Today, it is used in mouthwash and chewing gum.

✻ Purple coneflower

A traditional medicinal plant of Native American tribes living in the Great Plains, it was used to heal wounds, to remedy insect and snake bites, and indeed to cure most ailments.

✻ Ginseng

Its root has been used by traditional Chinese medicine for thousands of years. It is gathered so intensively that its population in the wild is under threat. For this reason, it is grown in fields, where it needs a lot of care.

Culinary herbs & spices

They contain aromatic substances that give food and drink the right taste and aroma. We use various parts of culinary herbs, notably the leaves, flowers, tops, fruit, and seeds. Herbs and spices are sold most commonly in dried form. But if we grow them at home in plant pots, we always have fresh herbs on hand.

Basil

Clove

Caraway

Marjoram

Saffron crocus

✹ Basil

The leaves of this herb are used as a seasoning, not least in Mediterranean cuisine. It's very popular on pizza and in pasta dishes, often in combination with tomatoes. Basil is sometimes referred to as the queen of herbs.

✹ Saffron crocus

Saffron is the world's most expensive spice: its stigmas are harvested only by hand. As each flower has two or three stigmas, it takes a very long time to harvest so much as a pound of this spice.

✹ Caraway

The use of caraway seeds has a very long history. Caraway is good for digestion and protects against flatulence. It is added to bread dough, boiled potatoes, roast meat, and many other dishes.

✳ Clove

Cloves are undeveloped buds of the tropical clove tree. They are harvested as soon as they begin to turn red, after which they are dried in the sun. Cloves are a good disinfectant and relieve toothache.

✳ Black pepper

Peppercorns are among the most commonly used spices. They can be black, white, or red—all come from the same plant. The difference comes from the ripeness of the corns and how they have been processed.

✳ Cardamom

The original home of the cardamom plant is the tropical rainforests of India, and it is there that the fruits and rhizomes of this sturdy plant are most popular as a spice.

Black pepper

Cardamom

Ginger

Flat-leaved vanilla

29

✳ Marjoram

Only the tip and undeveloped buds of the marjoram plant are used as a spice. Marjoram was once associated with the goddess of love Aphrodite, who was said to have created it as a symbol of happiness.

✳ Flat-leaved vanilla

This orchid is grown for its fruit, known as the vanilla pod. The fruit is harvested before ripening for further processing, as ripe fruit tends to burst, thereby releasing the fragrant matter.

✳ Ginger

Only the rhizome of the ginger plant is used as a spice. Indispensable for Asian cuisine, it has a fairly sharp taste. Not only is it used in meat and sweet dishes, but it is used for soft drinks too.

Field crops

These plants are grown in fields in large amounts. They are used for the nourishment of humans and the feeding of farm animals. In large fields, we come across various cereals (like wheat, barley, and rye), sunflowers, poppies, soybean plants, potatoes, and many other crops. As these are often staple foods, we encounter them every day on our plates. Industrial crops, such as fibers, are cultivated too.

Common wheat

Quinoa

Common sunflower

Cassava

❋ Common wheat

Along with rice and corn, wheat is one of the most important crops. Indeed, it is a staple food for a third of humanity. Wheat grain is used in bread, pastries, and pasta.

❋ Cassava

After decomposition, its tubers contain poisonous cyanide. The cyanide is removed by long soaking in water or fermentation; only once this has been done can cassava (or the flour prepared from it) be eaten.

❋ Quinoa

The Inca, the aboriginal people of the mountains of South America, ground quinoa into flour for bread. Today, quinoa is a staple food of their descendants. It is highly nutritious.

Asian rice

Rice comes in numerous shapes and colors—in its unpeeled state, it can be brown, red, purple, or even black. Most rice is grown in irrigated fields known as paddies, although some varieties are cultivated without irrigation.

Sugarcane

Sugarcane can grow to be 20 feet high. After being harvested, it is chopped up and pressed. The juice thus obtained is boiled several times before being rapidly cooled. Cane sugar then crystallizes on the surface of the juice.

Maize

Maize grain is used to make flour, starch, and oil, and also popcorn and cornflakes. In Mexico, its country of origin, it is included in many dishes. It is also an important foodstuff for livestock.

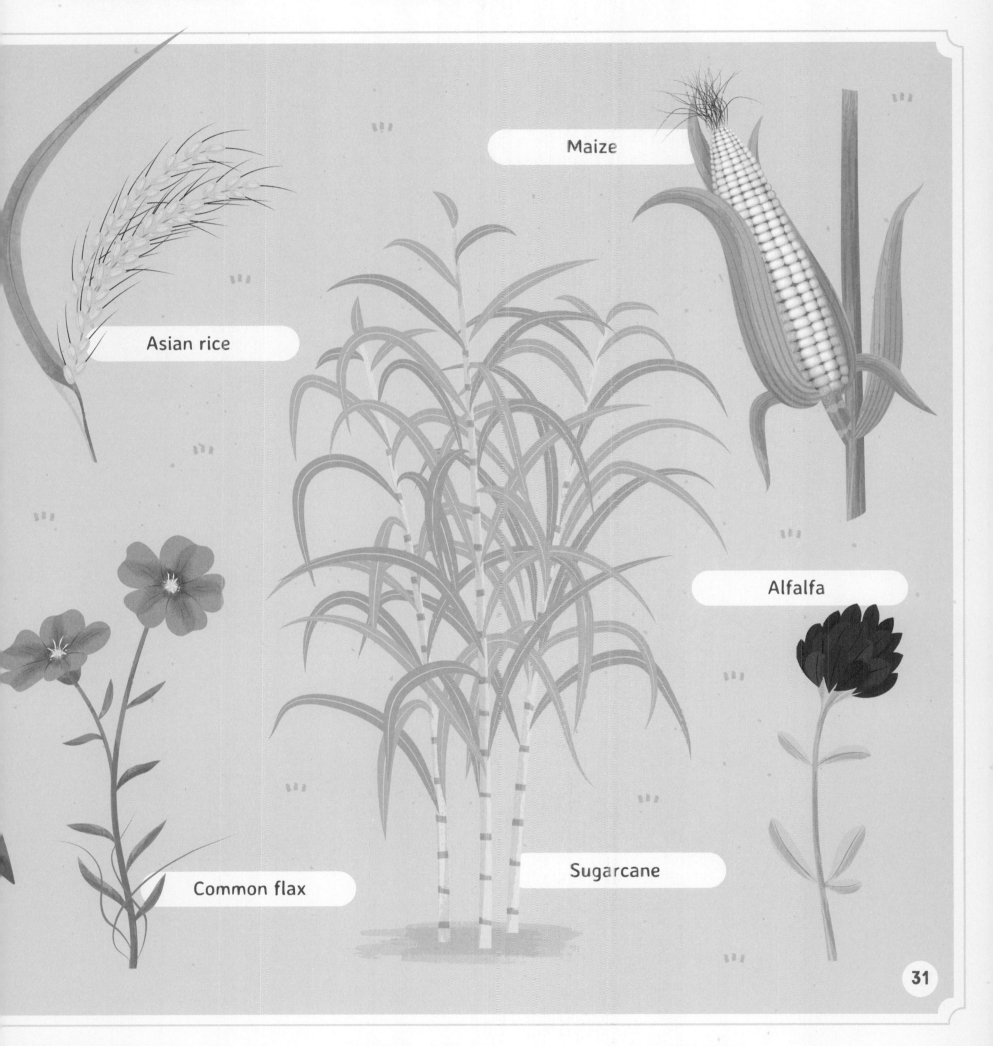

Maize

Asian rice

Alfalfa

Common flax

Sugarcane

Common sunflower

In daytime, the sunflower turns its head toward the sun. Sunflower seeds are very tasty, for humans and birds alike. The oil of sunflower seeds is used in cooking.

Common flax

A fiber for making fabrics (linen), sacks, and rope is obtained from stalks of the flax plant. In the distant past, the Ancient Egyptians wrapped the mummies of their Pharaohs in long strips of linen.

Alfalfa

This high-protein forage crop provides more than just feed for farm animals. After sprouting, its seeds contain a number of important substances that have a beneficial effect on the human body.

Vegetables

Vegetables have been part of the human diet since time immemorial. Like fruit, they are very good for our health. In fact, they are better still, as they have a lower sugar content. It is practically impossible to be unhealthy when it comes to vegetables! (Fried vegetables, however, aren't exactly low in fat.) Thanks to their wide range of tastes, vegetables liven up every meal while giving us the nutrients our health requires.

Carrot

Onion

Globe artichoke

Tomato

Brussels sprouts

✹ Carrot

The carrot is rich in beta-carotene, which the body turns into vitamin A. Everyone knows that carrots are orange. But for many years white, yellow, or purple carrots were more common.

✹ Globe artichoke

The buds of the artichoke are edible. Along with the tip of the stem, they are cut away while they are still green, before they come into bloom. They appeared as a delicacy on the plates of nobility in the Middle Ages.

✹ Tomato

The tomato is from America. When it first came to Europe, it was grown as an ornamental plant only. Later, people began to eat the fruit. Unripe, green tomatoes can cause poisoning.

✳ Onion

Most people cry when chopping onions. When the cells of an onion are breached, they release chemical substances that irritate our eyes. The eyes then produce tears to wash away the irritation.

✳ Horned melon

Also known as the kiwano, this melon originated in Africa. With its horn-like spines and orange skin, its fruit captures our attention at first sight. Under the skin is watery green flesh. It tastes rather like a cucumber.

✳ Capsicum

Wild species are spicy. They contain a substance that is hot to the taste for mammals, but not for birds. Birds are happy to eat the fruit of the capsicum. The seeds are then spread in bird droppings.

Horned melon

Capsicum

Beetroot

Squash

✳ Brussels sprouts

Brussels sprouts are hardy vegetables: they can withstand freezing temperatures. Indeed, having survived a freeze, they are even tastier.

✳ Beetroot

It cleanses the body, is good for liver function, activates the forming of red blood cells, works as an antioxidant and a diuretic, etc. If you ever eat a lot of beetroot, be forewarned: it will make your stools red.

✳ Squash

This enormous plant can produce tendrils over 30 feet long. The fruit of the squash is among the largest in the plant kingdom. In addition to being food, pumpkins (a kind of squash) are used to make jack-o'-lanterns.

Fruit crops

Most fruit crops are woody plants—i.e. trees and shrubs (bushes). In most cases, their fruit is sweet (the lemon, which is tart, is a notable exception). Fruit is a source of vitamins, minerals, and substances that are good for the human body. One warning, though: fruit also contains a lot of sugar. Although this sugar is natural, too much of it is not good for us.

Pomegranate

Banana plant

Golden kiwifruit

Wild strawberry

Pineapple

✹ Banana plant

The banana plant may look like a tree, but it is the world's largest herb, not a woody plant. Bananas are harvested before they ripen; they are then left to ripen in special rooms.

✹ Golden kiwifruit

This hairy brown fruit with green flesh—formally known as Actinidia chinensis—is high in vitamin C. This fruit's name refers to a bird from New Zealand called the kiwi, which it somewhat resembles.

✹ Wild strawberry

Wild strawberries are one of the most popular fruits all over the world. Although smaller than the strawberries grown in gardens, they have a more intense taste and smell. What's more, their roots, leaves, and fruits are medicinal.

✳ Pomegranate

The branches of this shrub or small tree are sometimes thorny. Its flowers are a striking red and its fruit is leathery. In its sweet yet tart flesh there are a great many seeds, which look like gemstones.

✳ Apricot

Having originated in China, the apricot tree has spread all over the world—even into space, when NASA astronauts took its fruit, in dried form, on an expedition. This fruit is exceptionally rich in substances that are good for our health.

✳ Blackberry

The thorny stems of this bush can give us a nasty scratch. But when we walk in the countryside, its black berries can provide us with a welcome refreshment. Also, its leaves can be used to make tea.

Blackberry

Apricot

Carica papaya

Apple

35

✳ Pineapple

The leaves of the pineapple are long and tough, their jagged edges sharp as a saw. They are arranged in a rosette, at whose center the fruit forms after flowering.

✳ Carica papaya

This herb can be 30 feet tall, with fruit weighing up to 20 pounds. It looks rather like a palm. We eat its sweet, juicy flesh. Its small seeds have a sharp, spicy taste and are used as a pepper substitute.

✳ Apple

Because of its fruit, this is one of the most commonly cultivated and popular fruit trees in the Temperate Zone. Did you know that apples float? Well, they do—owing to the fact that they are one-quarter air.

NON-FLOWERING PLANTS

These plants do not produce flowers, fruits, or seeds. They reproduce by means of spores. This group includes mosses, ferns, clubmosses, and horsetails. Mosses grow in damp, shady places such as rock and tree bark, and they do not mind the cold of mountainous areas. They retain water and protect the soil from drying out. Ferns, too, like shade and damp. New fern leaves are curled in spirals. Like clubmosses and horsetails, millions of years ago ferns helped to make black coal.

Luminous moss

It grows in cracks in rock and dark hollows between the roots of trees. Its protonema (the earliest stage of the life cycle, reminiscent of algae) glows greenish-yellow.

Pincushion moss

Shaped like cushions, it is silvery-green in color. In winters past, it was placed in windows as thermal insulation, as it prevented heat from escaping a room.

Common horsetail

In spring, a straight, brown stem, with a spikelet containing spores, sprouts from the ground. Once the spores have matured, the brown stem dries out, to be replaced by a green, summer stem.

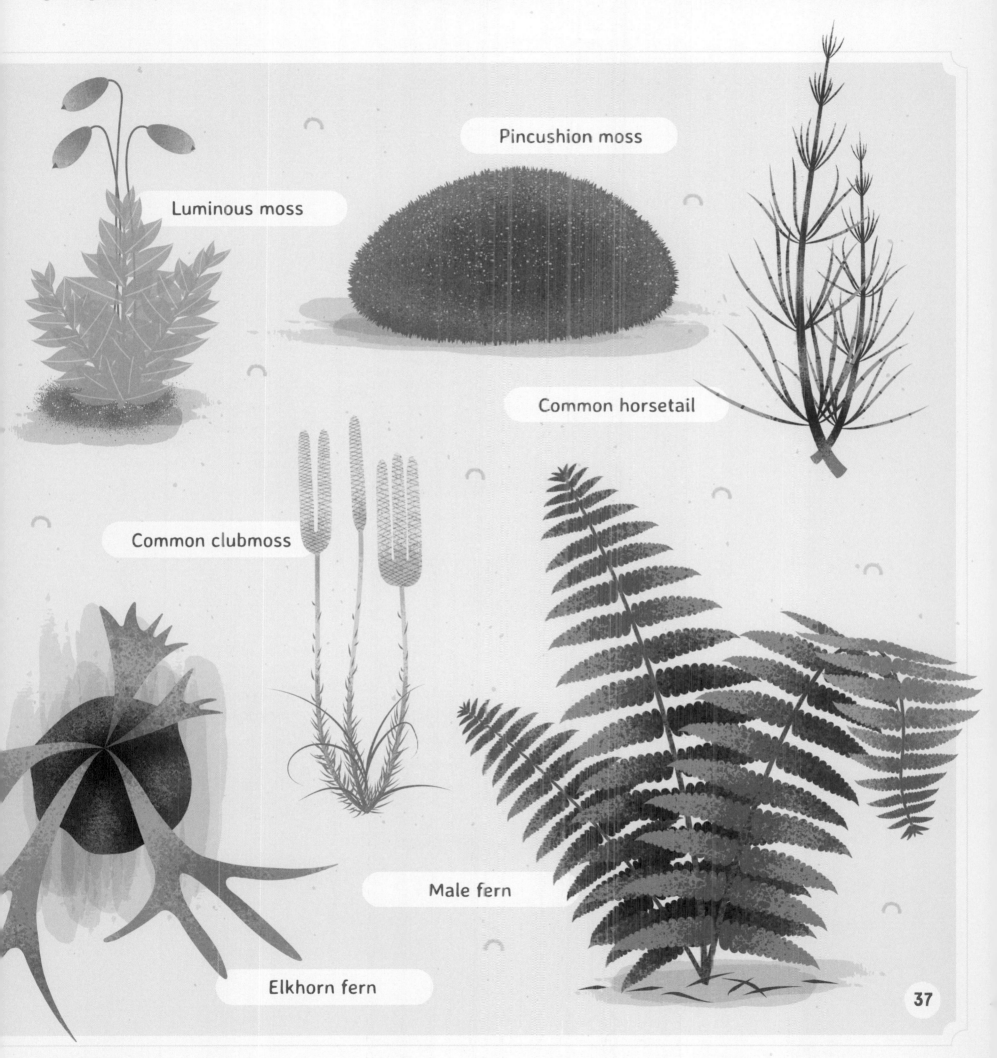

Pincushion moss

Luminous moss

Common horsetail

Common clubmoss

Male fern

Elkhorn fern

Elkhorn fern

This exotic fern has two types of leaves. The first resembles reindeer antlers and can grow to be three feet long. The second, round type attaches the plant firmly to the bark of a tree.

Common clubmoss

The clubmoss has a long, creeping, branched stem that is dotted with tiny leaves and ends in a hair-like white point. The spikes and spores are fork-shaped.

Male fern

You can't miss this robust fern, which can grow to be three feet high. It is found in most places of the world. Humans used to use it to protect themselves from intestinal parasites, notably the tapeworm.

FUNGI

Fungi are neither animals nor plants. In fact, they are a group of organisms in their own right. They have neither leaves nor flowers, nor do they contain chlorophyll. They take their nutrition from plants, both living and dead. A fungus has a cap, a stipe, and a mycelium. It reproduces by means of spores. Most fungi are found in woodlands, although we can also find them in meadows, gardens, and parks. Some fungi have weird and wonderful shapes. The best-known shape is the cap and stalk (stipe), but there are also fungi shaped like balls, bowls, tubes, even bushes. To grow, they need plenty of moisture.

✴ Netted stinkhorn

A lace net or stocking falls from beneath its cap, serving as protection against snails. It has an unpleasant taste and smell.

✴ Horn of plenty

Among the dry leaves and needles of the forest floor, this fungus looks like little black trumpets. Could they be the horns of woodland elves? They may not look very appealing, but they are edible.

✴ Jelly baby

More than anything, this orange fungus looks like a jelly-type canapé on a thick skewer.

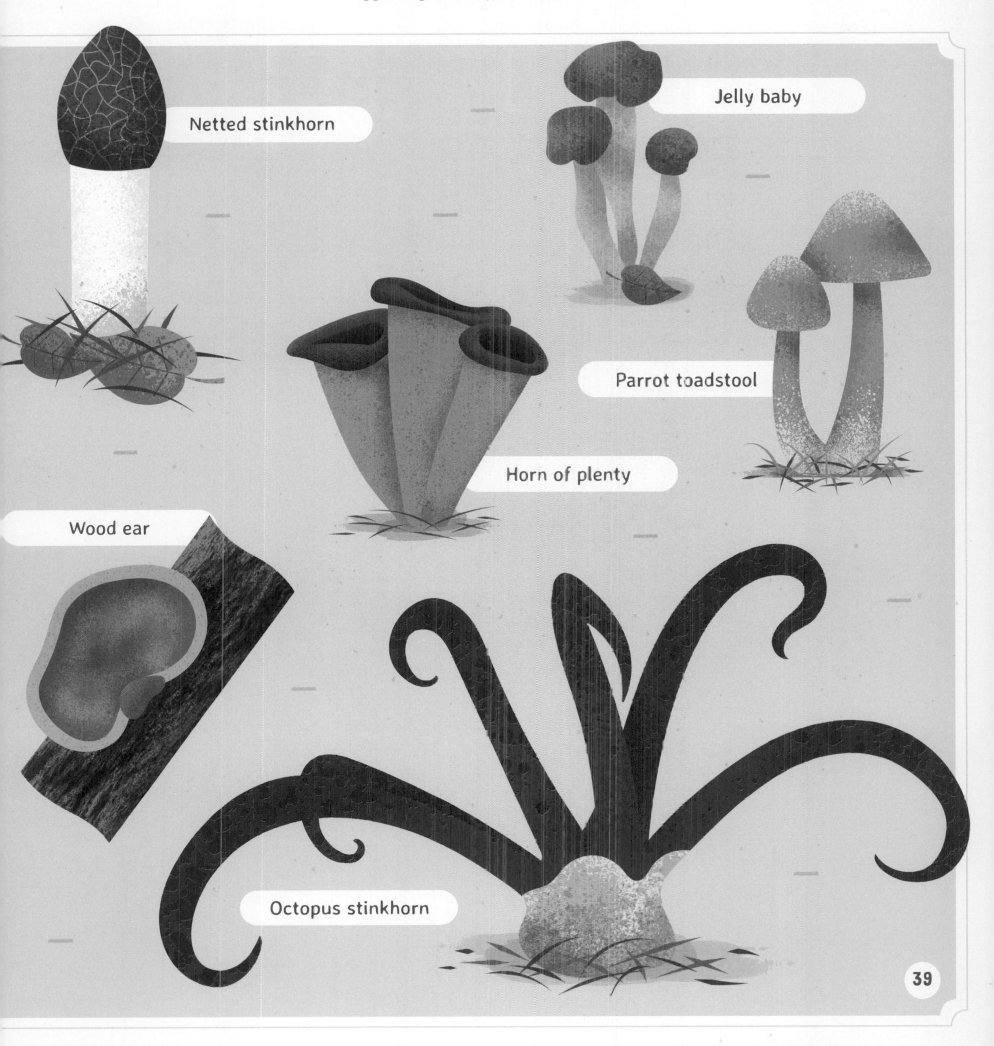

Netted stinkhorn

Jelly baby

Parrot toadstool

Horn of plenty

Wood ear

Octopus stinkhorn

✴ Wood ear

If you find a stem or a branch with ears, what you have is more than likely this mushroom. It grows on the living and dead wood of a deciduous tree, most commonly the elder. It is a popular ingredient in Asian cuisines.

✴ Octopus stinkhorn

This fungus comes from Australia. Its red arms, which look like octopus tentacles, are coated in smelly green slime.

✴ Parrot toadstool

The parrot toadstool has a yellow-green or green cap that is very slimy to the touch. We find it in meadows, pastureland, hillsides, and the grassy edges of woodlands.

Edible mushrooms

Edible mushrooms are an excellent food source. We can fry, roast, or pickle them, and we can add them to soups and sauces. Although most edible mushrooms are found in the wild, some, such as champignons and oyster mushrooms, are grown artificially.

Pearl oyster mushroom

Common morel

Truffle

Summer cep

Orange birch bolete

40

✳ Pearl oyster mushroom

It grows in large clumps on the stumps and trunks of deciduous trees. It is also grown in straw-filled sacks and on blocks of wood. It contains many health-promoting substances.

✳ Truffle

One of the most expensive foods in the world. It can be found as far as one foot below the ground. Trained dogs and pigs are used to find it: their sense of smell is more sensitive than a human's.

✳ Summer cep

One of the most sought-after mushrooms among mushroom pickers. Its cap of various shades of brown sits atop a tubby stipe. It grows in deciduous woodlands after heavy rains.

Common morel

The morel boasts a brownish cap with deep, irregular pits that often house insects or small animals.

Chanterelle

Lovers of mushroom delicacies can be glad that this beautiful, tasty, yellowy-orange mushroom is rarely eaten by worms. It grows among bilberries, moss, and tall grass in coniferous forests.

Common puffball

Although many puffballs are similar in shape, none but the common puffball has on its surface cone-shaped warts that can be easily rubbed off. If you press a ripe common puffball, it will send out a cloud of spores.

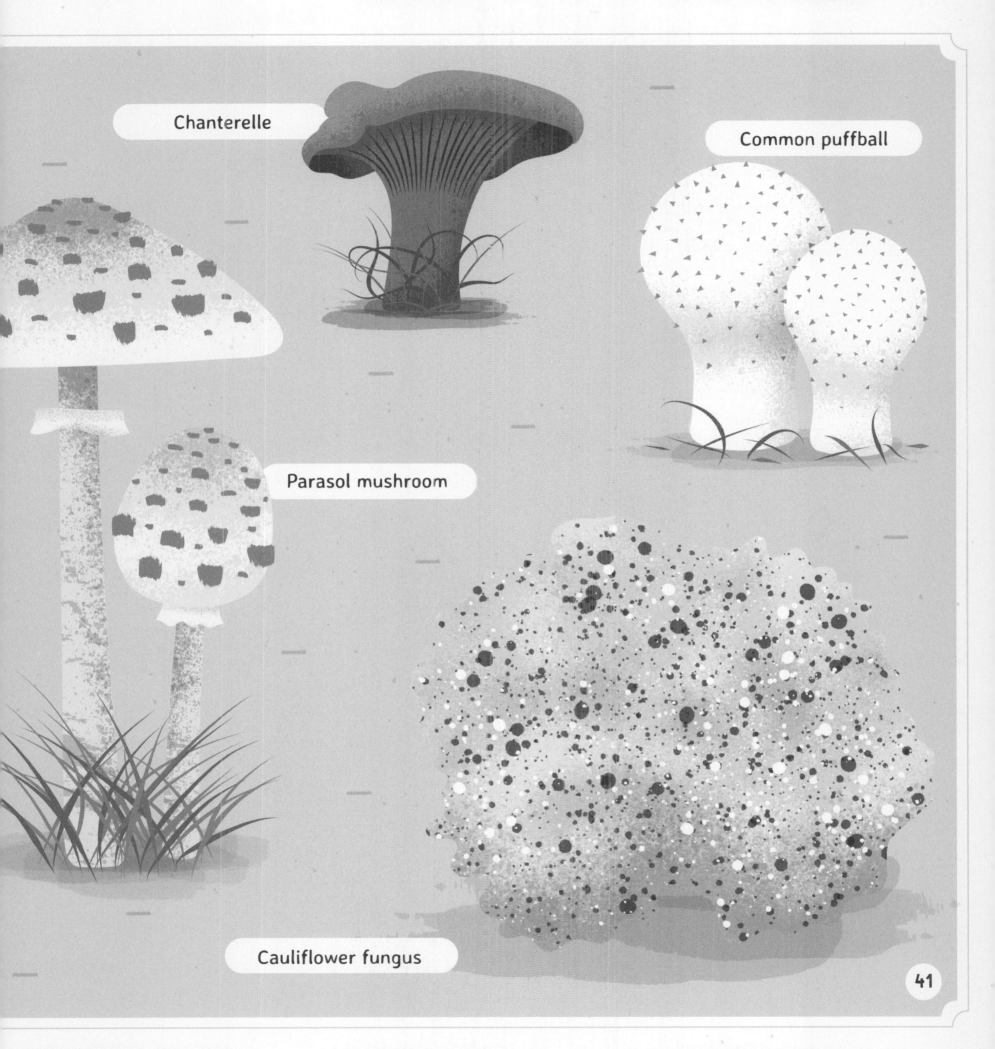

Chanterelle

Common puffball

Parasol mushroom

Cauliflower fungus

Orange birch bolete

The orange birch bolete likes to keep the birch tree company: we often find them next to each other. It has a yellow-orange cap and a white stipe dotted with small black scales.

Parasol mushroom

The cap has a scaly surface with a small brown bump in the middle. We find parasol mushrooms most commonly in tall grass, at the wayside, and on the edges of woodland.

Cauliflower fungus

This large mushroom is made up of curly lobes that twist this way and that. At first, its color is light. Over time, it changes from yellow to brown. It is found most commonly under pine trees.

Inedible mushrooms

These mushrooms are neither poisonous nor edible. Most of them taste disgusting. If we added them to our food, they would really spoil it. But at least they are pleasing to the eye.

Golden cup

Mycena strobilicola

Split-gill mushroom

Candlestick fungus

Ramariopsis pulchella

✳ Golden cup

At first, it is spherical in shape. Later, it will open to form a cup. Its inner surface is smooth and yellow-orange, while its outer surface is greenish-blue and grainy. It grows in spring, but we rarely find it.

✳ Split-gill mushroom

Its cap is shaped like a clam or a fan. Its gray-white surface is furry. A wood-decaying fungus, it grows on deciduous trees.

✳ Ramariopsis pulchella

It is comprised of thin purple branches. Rare, it grows on the ground of light deciduous woodland, at the wayside, in scrub, and in meadows.

✳ Mycena strobilicola

This small mushroom has a brown or gray-brown cap. It grows on rotting spruce cones, which are at least partially buried in the ground, or on needles.

✳ Magpie fungus

The spontaneous decomposition of the cap is characteristic of mushrooms of this genus. By turning its cap into a black mush, the magpie fungus can flow down a hillside, thereby spreading its spores.

✳ Red belt conk

This abundant, hard, tough fungus attaches to wood like a shelf. The youngest of its layers is orange-yellow with a white margin. The oldest layer is black or gray.

Magpie fungus

Red belt conk

Fringed earthstar

Bleeding tooth fungus

43

✳ Candlestick fungus

It has antler-like branches. Its lower black part contrasts with its upper white part. It grows plentifully on tree stumps and dead trunks and branches of deciduous trees.

✳ Fringed earthstar

The most interesting thing about the earthstar is its shape. It begins as a ball, which matures to split open, forming several rays and revealing inside a sac filled with spores.

✳ Bleeding tooth fungus

It grows under spruces and pines in coniferous woodland, and it is rare. In wet conditions, its velvety white cap is adorned with blood-red drops.

Poisonous mushrooms

Poisonous mushrooms contain toxins, which, if taken in certain amounts, are harmful to human health and may even result in death. Some animals, such as snails, are happy to feast on these mushrooms, as they are untroubled by the poisonous substances.

Death cap

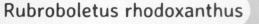
Rubroboletus rhodoxanthus

Satan's bolete

Freckled dapperling

✳ Rubroboletus rhodoxanthus

Some experts consider Rubroboletus rhodoxanthus the most beautiful of all bolete mushrooms. Its light-gray cap sits atop a bulbous yellow stem covered with a dense, strikingly red net pattern.

✳ Satan's bolete

Its very name is enough to put you off. It has a very pale gray-white cap above red tubes; the stem—or stipe—is red too. Eaten raw, even a small piece of this mushroom may cause poisoning.

✳ Freckled dapperling

Its cream-brown cap is embellished with striking spines. It has an unpleasant smell and tastes slightly sour. We find it in gardens and parks, on the roadside, and in woodlands.

✹ Death cap

One of the most poisonous mushrooms in the world. It grows from an egg shape, which in adult specimens becomes distinctly chalice-shaped. In most cases, the cap is a striking bright green, with a hint of olive green.

✹ Violet crown-cup

It begins in the ground as a spherical, hollow mushroom. Once it has partially emerged from the surface, it opens to form a cup, the inner surface of which is purple. The outer surface is white or purplish.

✹ Brain mushroom

Its dark-brown cap may remind you of a withered brain. We often find it in spring, mostly in coniferous woodland.

Violet crown-cup

Brain mushroom

American yellow fly agaric

Fly agaric

Steel-blue entoloma

✹ American yellow fly agaric

This glowing yellow toadstool is typically found in certain regions of North America. On rare occasions, we find it elsewhere too.

✹ Fly agaric

Do you know this one? I expect you do. With its lovely coloring, this mushroom looks splendid in the woods. It is one of the best-known and best-looking poisonous mushrooms.

✹ Steel-blue entoloma

The steel-blue entoloma grows individually or in small groups in coniferous woodland. It is characterized by its metallic blue color.

LICHENS

It may seem that a lichen is one organism, but this is not so. While most of it is made up of fungus, a smaller part is comprised of algae, or cyanobacteria, in a mutually beneficial coexistence: the fungus supplies water and minerals, while the algae (cyanobacteria) produces—by means of green dyes and sunlight—complex energy-giving substances. Lichens can live in very inhospitable conditions (for example, in high mountains, polar regions, and deserts). They are sensitive to polluted environments, however.

Old man's beard

Old man's beard grows mainly on trees. Thanks to its stringy appearance, it reminds us of gray or greenish hair. Sometimes it hangs from a tree in a continuous curtain.

Reindeer lichen

A gray, shrubby lichen. In polar regions, it is an important source of food for reindeer, which graze on large quantities of it.

Common orange lichen

Common orange lichen is widespread on rocky shores, house walls, tree bark, and cliffs. In direct sunlight it is yellowy-orange, but in the shade it is yellowy-green.

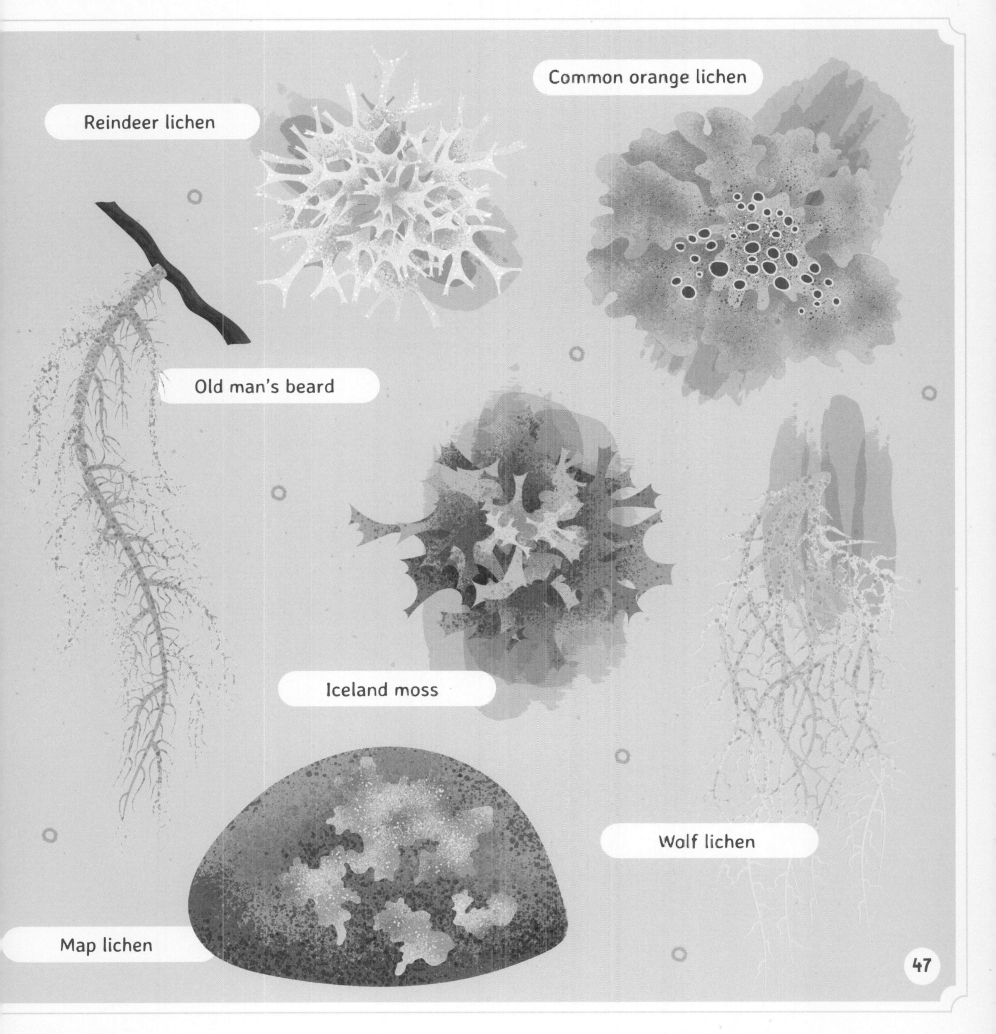

Common orange lichen

Reindeer lichen

Old man's beard

Iceland moss

Wolf lichen

Map lichen

47

Map lichen

These yellowish-green patches with black edging are often found on rock, making shapes on it that look like maps.

Iceland moss

With its healing properties, Iceland moss contains substances that help in the treatment of certain illnesses (like coughs and infections of the respiratory tract). It, too, provides food for reindeer.

Wolf lichen

This striking, yellowish-green, shrubby lichen settles naturally on the bark of coniferous trees. It contains a poisonous substance that was once used to kill wolves and foxes.

Encyclopedia of Plants, Fungi, and Lichens

for Young Readers

Written by Tereza Němcová
Illustrated by Tomáš Pernický

© Designed by B4U Publishing for Albatros,
an imprint of Albatros Media Group, 2022.
5. května 22, Prague 4, Czech Republic.
Printed in Ukraine by Unisoft.

www.albatrosbooks.com

ISBN: 978-80-00-06351-5